TO MY GODDAMN KIDS! I LOVE YOU — P.B.

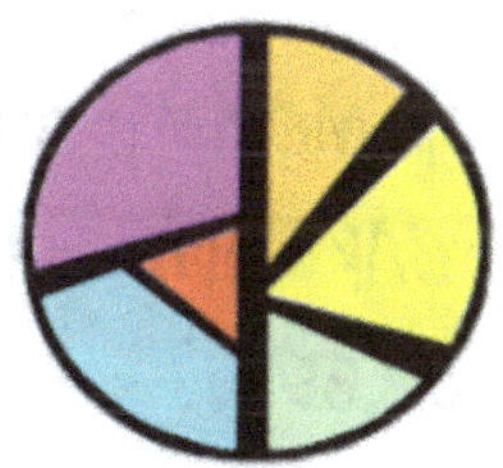

WRITE THE AUTHOR
AT
PAULBLAKERBOOKS.COM

The seed for this book was planted firmly in the soil of reality—this vacuum cleaner incident unfortunately being true...

Our little guy took mommy's fun, new expression to daycare and shared it with his friends. They liked it!

After our apologies, others confessed secret 'baby's first swear words' too. You'll find several true pages within.

I hope this book will help make light of a funny childhood milestone, that often makes it into family folklore. There's a page to add your own at the end. Enjoy!

(Names of stuffies have been changed to protect the innocent.)

HOLY SHIT, IT'S BOBO!

RIGHT IN THE FRIGGIN' NUTS, MOMMY!

DIRECTIONS
WHADDA PIECE OF SHIT!

FUCK MY LIFE
TOO, MOMMY !

OH, CRAP!
OH, CRAP!
DAMN DOGS
NEWS

NICKY HAD FUN ON FISHING TRIPS
WITH HIS UNCLE MIKE. HE LEARNED
MORE THAN HOW TO JUST BAIT A
HOOK AND CATCH A FISH, HE
LEARNED HOW TO STEER THE BOAT
AND FIND A GOOD FISHING SPOT. HE
LEARNED ALL ABOUT UNCLE MIKE'S
COLORFUL LURES—AND HIS
COLORFUL LANGUAGE. BEST OF ALL,
HE LEARNED HOW TO 'ZIP IT' ON THE
GROWN UP WORDS, FOR CANDY
BRIBES.

IS IT ANOTHER BIG FUCKER, UNCLE MIKE?!

MENU
I'M NOT THROWING A SHIT FIT!

SHUT THE HELL UP!
SHUT THE HELL UP!
SHUT THE HELL UP!

Little Bella had the best nanny ever! Ms. Lola sang songs and played dolls and even cooked yummy lunches! But at three o'clock, Bella's nanny hated to miss her favorite tele-novela.

Bella learned all sorts of new words when **VIDA DE FANTASIA** was on. At bedtime, her mama would be a bit surprised when her sweetie pie asked, 'Are there any putas under the bed?'

PUTA ?
SLAP!
62

YES, STOP BEING A DIPSHIT, MR. MITTENS!

#*&%$@!?!
TIMMY, STOP SAYING THAT!
THE WORST WORD YOU CAN EVER IMAGINE!

Bob had reluctantly clicked 'Kids OK' on his dating app, but there were signs that he might not be cut out for it.

Little Max wouldn't be the last kid to try and master one of Bob's funny sounding words — and Jenny(36) would get a clue why Bob might still be single when she got back from the bathroom.

HEY, YOU LITTLE MOTHER FUCKER!
...MOTHER
FLORIDA
FU
UNIVERSITY
GRAP

EAT THIS, BUTT FACE!
SUCK TURDS!
DIE SCUMBAG, DIE!
SCORE

WHAT DA FUCK, NOAH?

YEAH, THANKS A LOT NUMBNUTS!

GODDAMNIT!!

After the game, little Carter
called the cat, then grandma,
a dumbass.
Dad tried to blame his
football buddy, but mom
wasn't buying it—she'd
already given her hubby a
20 yard penalty for calling
the ref a jerkoff in the first
quarter.

GRRR....
NICE KICK, DUMBASS

ALL DA BITCHES IN DA HOUSE, SAY HO!

Sophie's Salon
YEAH MOMMY, WHAT A PRICK!

CANNONBALL!!!
FLIPPIN' BUTT MUNCH!

BITCHIN'!
FUCKIN' RAD, DUDE!
I LOVE CARROTS!
OCEAN BEACH SKAT
RULES OF USE:

OUCH!
OUCH!
HOLY SHIT!!
#1 DAD

IT SEEMS INUIT FOLK ARE GENERALLY NOT KNOWN FOR THIER POTTY MOUTHS. BUT I BET THERE MUST HAVE BEEN A TIME OR TWO, WHEN THE SLED TIPPED OVER IN A STORM, OR THE DOG ATE A FAVORITE MITTEN, OR THEY COULDN'T GET THE PACKERS GAME ON THE SATELLITE DISH..?

(FUCKING DOG)

WHY WAS GRAMPA'S
BUSINESS PARTNER
A, 'NO GOOD, LYING,
SHIT WEASEL,
DOUCHE BAG?'
VISITOR`S DAY

FUUUUUCK!!
7
7

UGH !!!
HELL DAY, HELL DAY, LA, LA, LAA....

BEACH DAY SUCKS ASS !!

Once you think you've mastered not swearing at home, try car swearing. Over 70% of all babies first swear words are car related (probably?) Classical music and biting down on the seatbelt are good techniques to help deal with these times.

NICE DRIVING, ASSHOLE!
(JIM WAS HAVING A BAD DAY.)

BLOODY LITTLE BASTARDS!

FUCK YEAH
...OH BABY!

BITE ME, TOO!

...SO I TOLD MY BOSS TO KISS MY ASS!
HEHEHE, KISS MY ASS

SANTA VISIT
(ANY MALL, U.S.A.)

MOMMY, WHAT'S A CLUSTERFUCK?!

SOMETIMES YOU ARE JUST OUT
TRYING TO SURPRISE YOUR WIFE
WITH SATURDAY MORNING DONUTS.
THEN YOUR ANGEL DROPS HER DOLL
UNDER THE SEAT. THEN YOU DRIVE
THROUGH A STOP SIGN TRYING TO
FISH IT OUT. THEN THIS HAPPENS...
SOMETIMES DONUTS COST $275.

WHAT DOES OFFICER DICKWAD WANT, DADDY?
POLICE
VIOLATION

I CAN'T SEE SHIT EITHER, DAD!

DRAW YOUR OWN
BABY'S FIRST SWEAR WORD
(WHEN IT HAPPENS TO YOU, TOO!)

DATE:

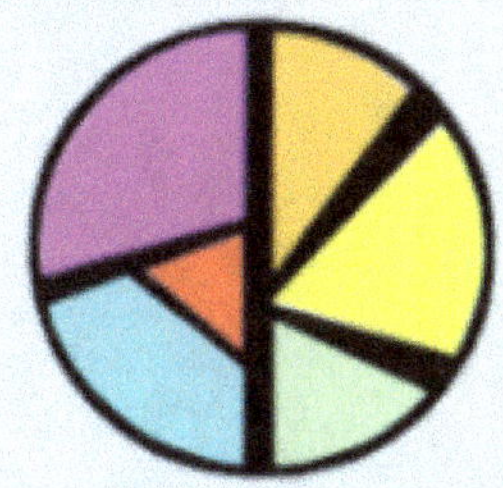

PAULBLAKERBOOKS.COM

The author would like to thank the other parents who shared a funny story to help inspire this book, and the people who have kept encouraging me along the way. The images were created digitally using GIMP open source image editor. Bubble font: Timotheos. Cover font: Dirty Brush. Self published in the U.S.A.

9 780578 335384